Date: 4/29/19

BR 005.1 NOL
Noll, Elizabeth,
Coding in the Internet /

CODING IS EVERYWHERE

Coding in the Internet

by Elizabeth Noll

BELLWETHER MEDIA • MINNEAPOLIS, MN

Note to Librarians, Teachers, and Parents:

Blastoff! Readers are carefully developed by literacy experts and combine standards-based content with developmentally appropriate text.

Level 1 provides the most support through repetition of high-frequency words, light text, predictable sentence patterns, and strong visual support.

Level 2 offers early readers a bit more challenge through varied simple sentences, increased text load, and less repetition of high-frequency words.

Level 3 advances early-fluent readers toward fluency through increased text and concept load, less reliance on visuals, longer sentences, and more literary language.

Level 4 builds reading stamina by providing more text per page, increased use of punctuation, greater variation in sentence patterns, and increasingly challenging vocabulary.

Level 5 encourages children to move from "learning to read" to "reading to learn" by providing even more text, varied writing styles, and less familiar topics.

Whichever book is right for your reader, Blastoff! Readers are the perfect books to build confidence and encourage a love of reading that will last a lifetime!

This edition first published in 2019 by Bellwether Media, Inc.

No part of this publication may be reproduced in whole or in part without written permission of the publisher. For information regarding permission, write to Bellwether Media, Inc., Attention: Permissions Department, 6012 Blue Circle Drive, Minnetonka, MN 55343.

Library of Congress Cataloging-in-Publication Data

Names: Noll, Elizabeth, author.
Title: Coding in the Internet / by Elizabeth Noll.
Description: Minneapolis, MN : Bellwether Media, Inc., 2019. | Series:
   Blastoff! Readers. Coding Is Everywhere | Includes bibliographical
   references and index. | Audience: Ages 5 to 8. | Audience: Grades K to 3.
Identifiers: LCCN 2017059997 (print) | LCCN 2017060779 (ebook) | ISBN
   9781626178342 (hardcover : alk. paper) | ISBN 9781618914781
   (pbk. : alk. paper) | ISBN 9781681035758 (ebook)
Subjects: LCSH: Internet programming–Juvenile literature.
Classification: LCC QA76.625 (ebook) | LCC QA76.625 .N65 2019 (print) | DDC
   006.7/6–dc23
LC record available at https://lccn.loc.gov/2017059997

Editor: Christina Leaf   Designer: Brittany McIntosh

Printed in the United States of America, North Mankato, MN

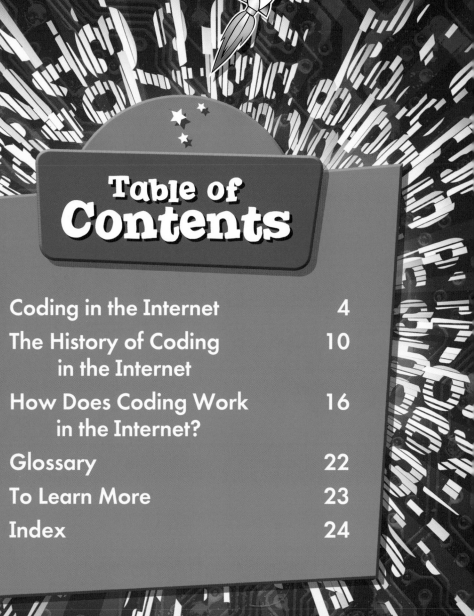

Table of Contents

Coding in the Internet

Do you listen to music on the **Internet**? Do you watch videos on YouTube? Maybe you find web sites about favorite animals.

Every web site you see was built with **code**!

Code tells computers what to do.

Everything on a web site is created with code. It controls how things look and move.

What Coding Creates on a Web Site

navigation menu

logo

web address

site content

Code uses the English language. But it looks different from what you write.

HTML and CSS

Simple web site in HTML:

code

web site

Simple web site in CSS:

code

web site

It is written in special computer languages. These include **HTML** and **CSS**.

The History of Coding in the Internet

computer room in the 1960s

Early computers could not share information with one another.

In the 1960s, the United States military figured out how. It created an early form of the Internet.

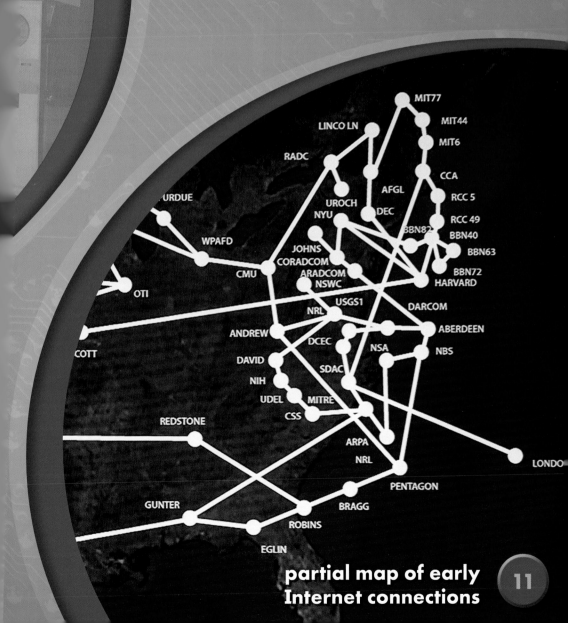

partial map of early Internet connections

Tim Berners-Lee, creator of the World Wide Web

In the 1980s, other people started using the Internet.

Then a scientist created the **World Wide Web**. Most people use the Internet through the Web.

the first web site

The World Wide Web project

info.cern.ch/hype

World Wide Web

The WorldWideWeb (W3) is a wide-area hypermedia infor

Everything there is online about W3 is linked directly or in

What's out there?
    Pointers to the world's online information, subjects ,
Help
    on the browser you are using
Software Products
    A list of W3 project components and their current sta
Technical
    Details of protocols, formats, program internals etc
Bibliography
    Paper documentation on W3 and references
People
    A list of some people involved in the project.

HTML was the first Web language.

HTML

14

partial map showing
Internet connections today

Today there are hundreds of computer languages. They make it easy to create web sites!

Say you e-mail a photo of your drawing to your grandma. How does code help?

The e-mail and photo are lines of code.

E-mail to Code

e-mail to Grandma:

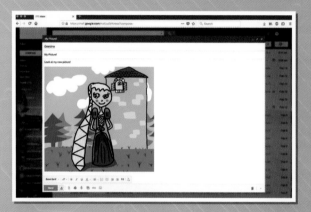

sample of e-mail in code:

```
:parseInt(h[1],10))||ab(0==g[2].length,0==h[2].length)||ab(g[2],h[
;if(38==g||63==g)if(g=b.charCodeAt(c+f),!g||61==g||38==g||35==g)r
2d[b]:d[b]=c(b)},jb={},P=function(b){return kb(b,function(){return
q--){var n=b.charAt(q),l=h[n];if("undefined"==typeof l)throw Erro
.join("")}var na=c(g)}catch(Za){return b}return-1==na.indexOf("thr
}return Aa;if(rb)return O()||y("iPad")||y("iPod")?R(/CriOS\/([0-9
earTimeout(b.b);d(c)};ub(this)};vb.prototype.g=function(){this.c
turn c&&!Ab(b)||!c&&!/(^[0-9A-F]*$)|(^[0-9a-f]*$)/.test(b)},Ab=fu
||ua&&P(Fb)||va&&P("522")||sa&&P("9.5")}}Cb=Db?null:t.GM_MOOSE_UR
1");Kb=!0}var Pb;if(Pb=fb("th")&&fb("view")){var Qb=gb("view");Pb
b(W)||Q(W)||(ac=ac.replace(W,mb(W)));var bc=cb($b,ac),cc=bc.index
r Z=new vb;v("GM_LP",Z.j);v("GM_SLP",Z.g.bind(Z));v("GM_SLC",Z.f.
' ]]></script><style nonce="8RXwbwuoeDVdbzo6Sq+vKyVEYIg">
ody{margin:0;width:100%;height:100%} body,td,input,textarea,select
'style><style nonce="8RXwbwuoeDVdbzo6Sq+vKyVEYIg">
ubmit_as_link{border:none; background:none; color:blue;text-decor-
'style></head><body><div style="font-size:0;color:white;z-index:-9
oading {display:none}
'style><form action="?ui=html&amp;zy=c" method="post"><input type=
ocument.getElementById("reloadurl").onclick=function(){sc("GMAIL S
ar GLOBALS=[null,null,"186386752","gmail_fe_180214.11_p5","iEEFj79
/_/scs/mail-static/_/ss/k/x3dgmail.main.-2fhz8pstcwsx.L.F4.O/am/x3
p",[1000:500000,10,200000,5,100000,3,75000,2,0,1"],["h","https:/
adipi","https://ssl.gstatic.com/ui/v1/icons/mail/localized/en/adi
```

router

The computer puts this code into **packets**. Then it sends the packets to the **router**. The router's code sends the packets to Grandma's router.

E-mailing a Picture

type e-mail and attach photo

```
0011100010101000111100
1000011111101010101011
0110100110101010101110
1000110101000011000111
0101010100001110011010
1010011101011001110110
0011010101101011101010
```

code is wrapped into packet

code sends packet to router

router sends packet to other router

code sends packet to Grandma's e-mail

e-mail with the photo arrives!

Grandma's computer gets the packets from the router. She opens her e-mail and sees your drawing.

Code makes all this possible!

Glossary

code—instructions for a computer

CSS—short for Cascading Style Sheets; CSS is a language used to style text on web pages.

HTML—short for HyperText Markup Language; HTML is a language used for building web sites.

Internet—a communication system that connects computers and computer networks all over the world

packets—small pieces of information sent between computers

router—a tool that moves information from one computer network to another

World Wide Web—a part of the Internet that makes it easier to get from one site to another

To Learn More

AT THE LIBRARY

Kelly, James Floyd. *Coding*. New York, N.Y.: DK Publishing, 2017.

Kelly, James Floyd. *The Story of Coding*. New York, N.Y.: DK Publishing, 2017.

Lyons, Heather, and Elizabeth Tweedale. *Learn to Program*. Minneapolis, Minn.: Lerner Publications, 2017.

ON THE WEB

Learning more about coding in the Internet is as easy as 1, 2, 3.

1. Go to www.factsurfer.com.

2. Enter "coding in the Internet" into the search box.

3. Click the "Surf" button and you will see a list of related web sites.

With factsurfer.com, finding more information is just a click away.

Index